THE FIRE DRAGON

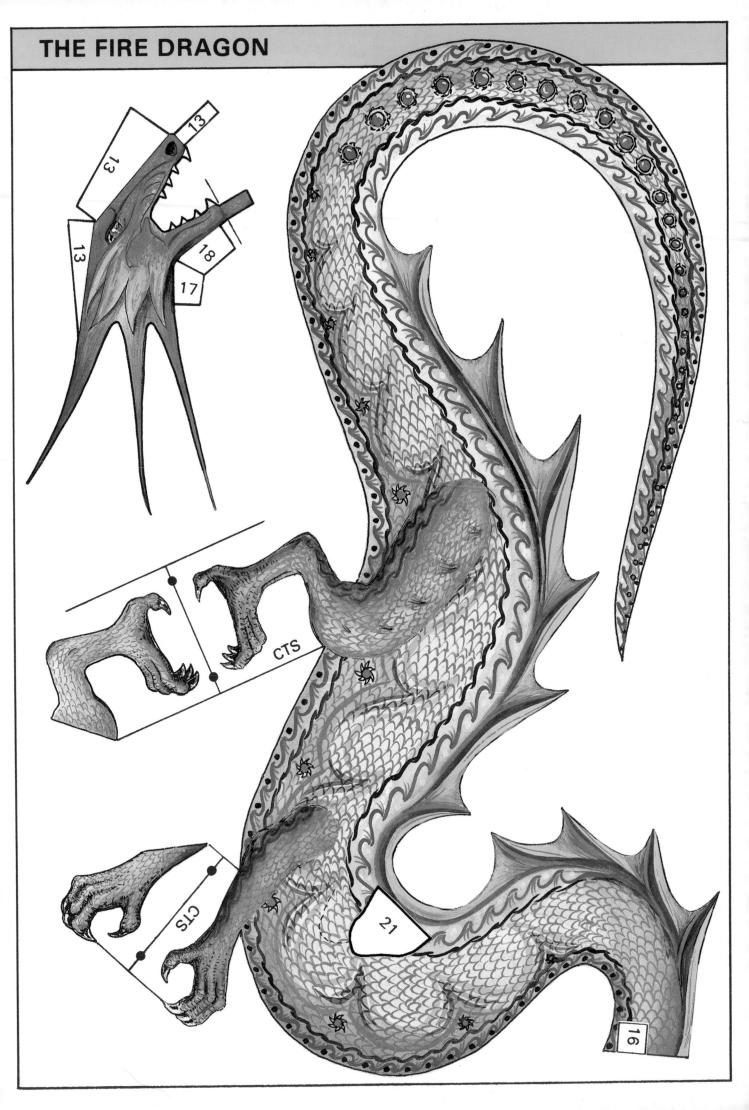

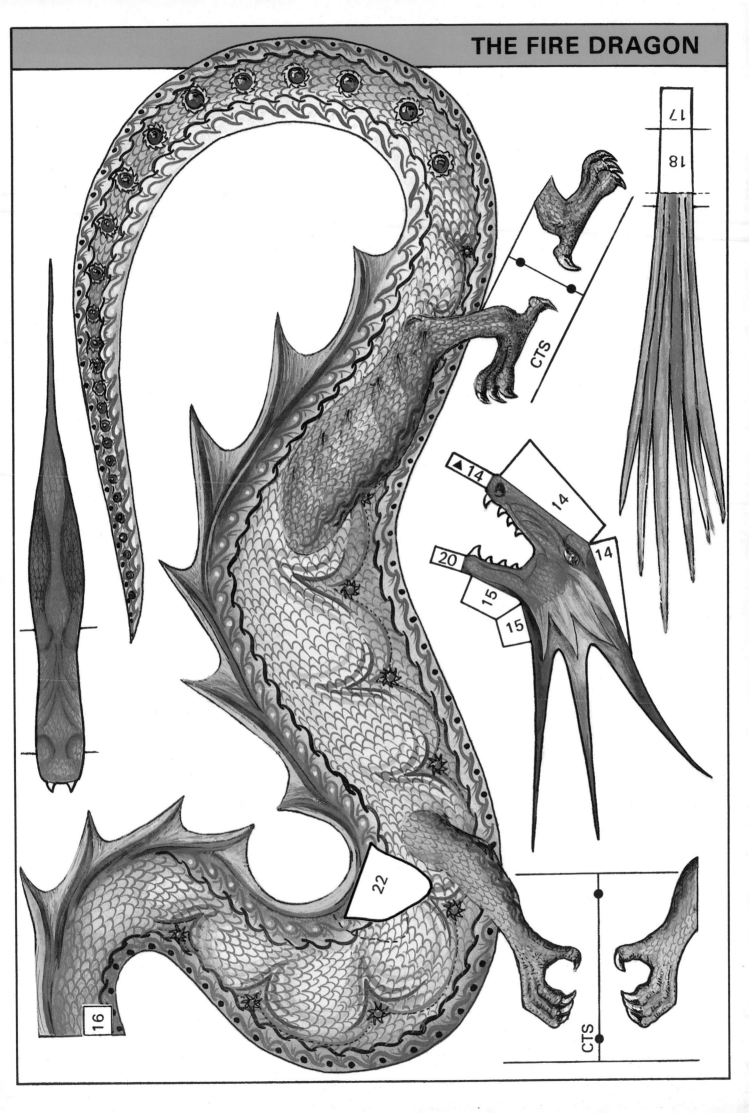

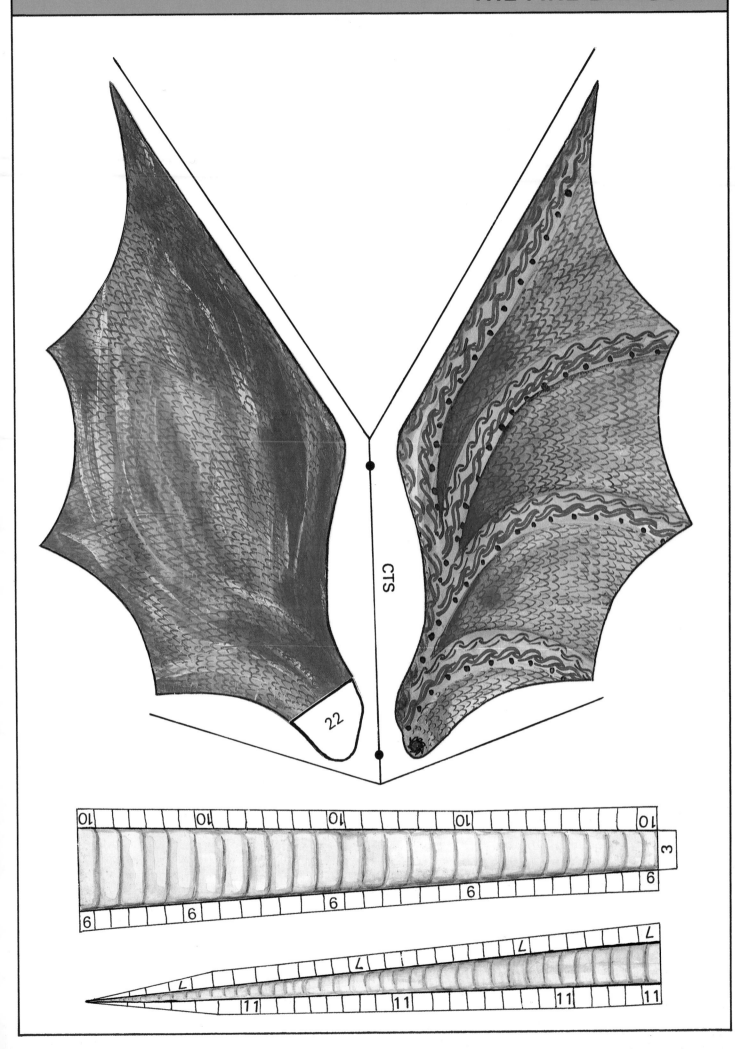

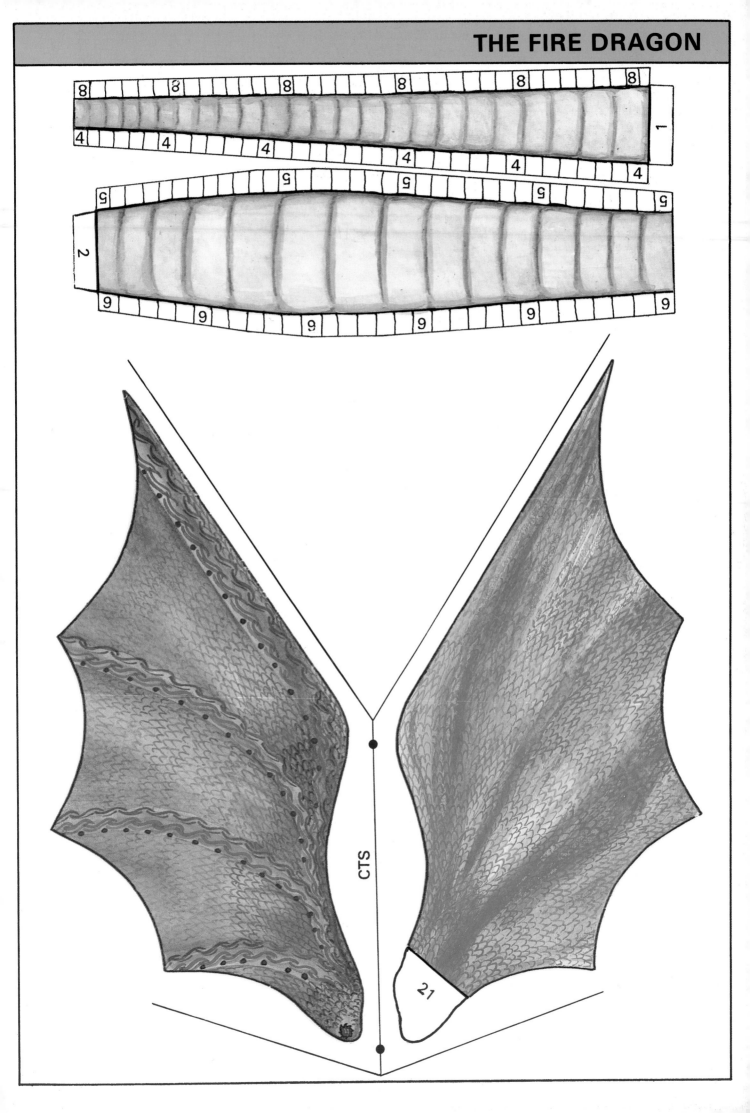

SPECIAL POINTS FOR THE 'ST GEORGE' SIDE

1. The black lines on the horse's body and legs are score lines. Score along them and then ease into gentle folds to give a slightly three dimensional appearance.

2. All the flaps are marked with letters of the alphabet. Work in order A,B,C, ... etc.

3. Finally glue the flaps marked * to the background and lightly glue the spear to the frame and the horse's front leg.

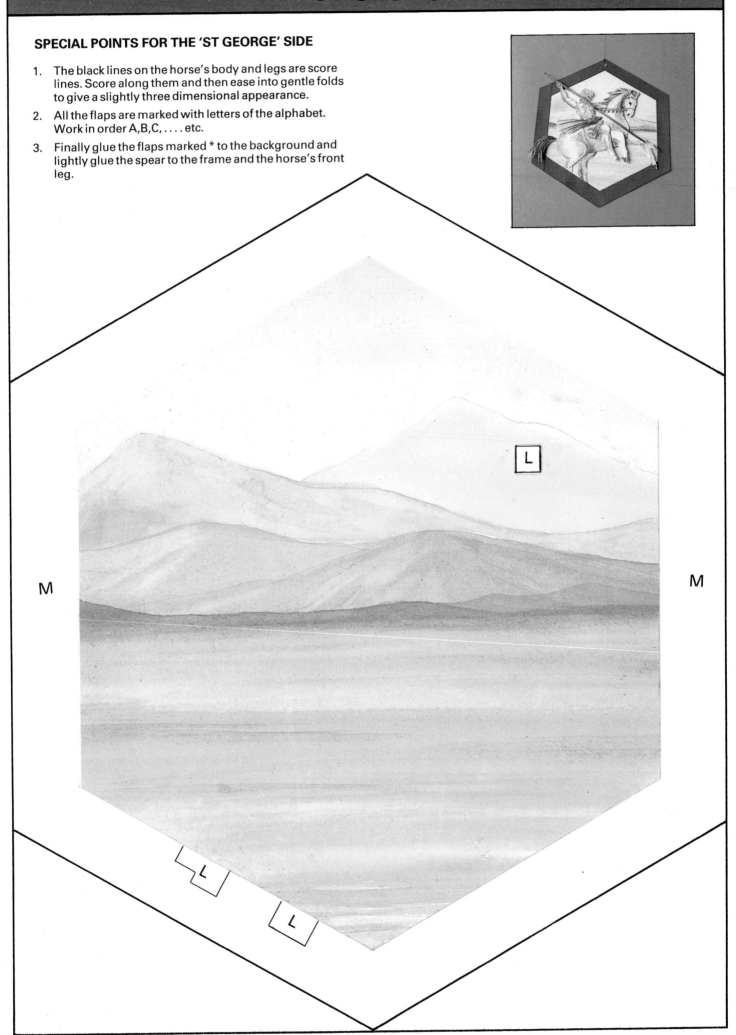

SPECIAL POINTS FOR THE 'DRAGON' SIDE

1. All the flaps are marked with numbers. Work in order 1,2,3, ... etc.
2. The black lines on the body, tail and wings are score lines. Score along them and then ease into gentle folds in order to give a slightly three dimensional appearance.
3. Gently curl the flames.

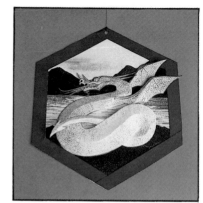

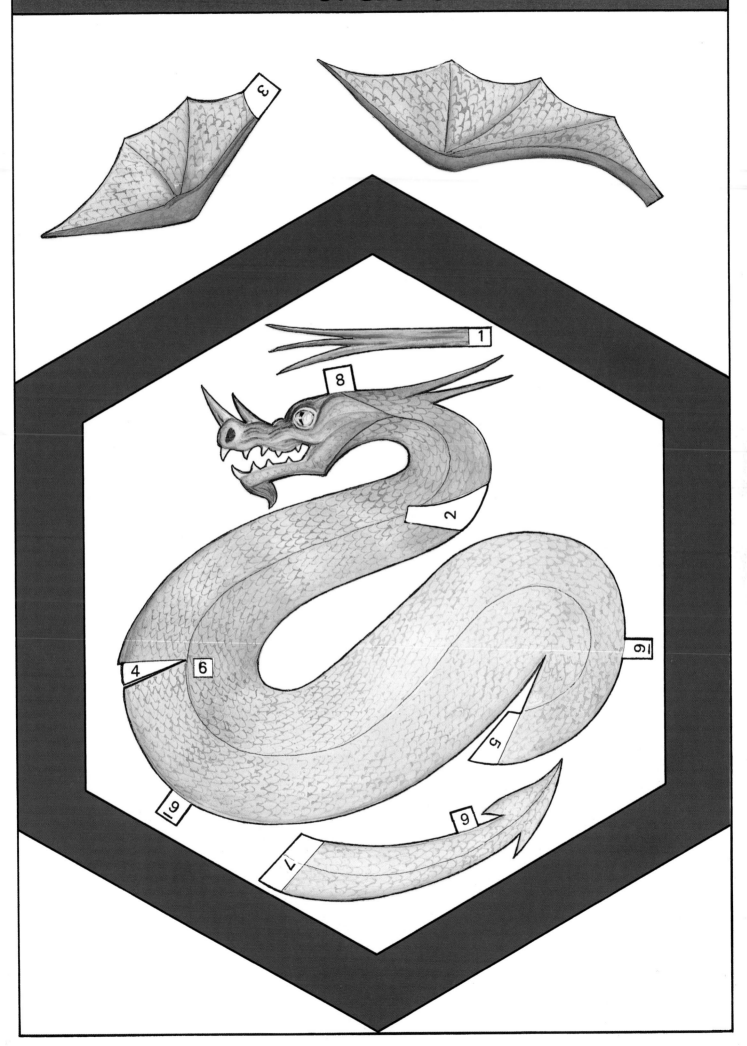

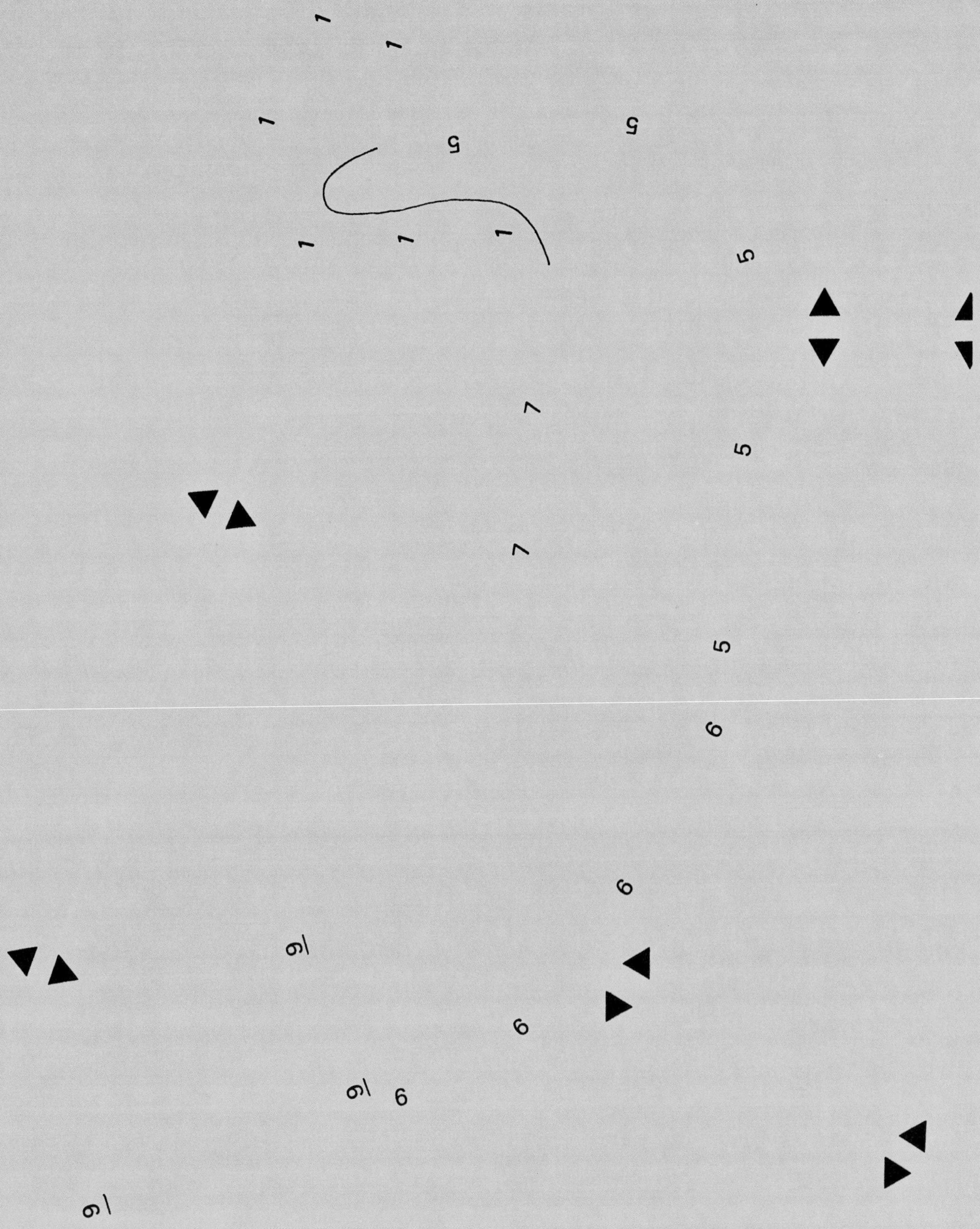

CTS

CTS

CTS

4 4 4

6 6 6 6

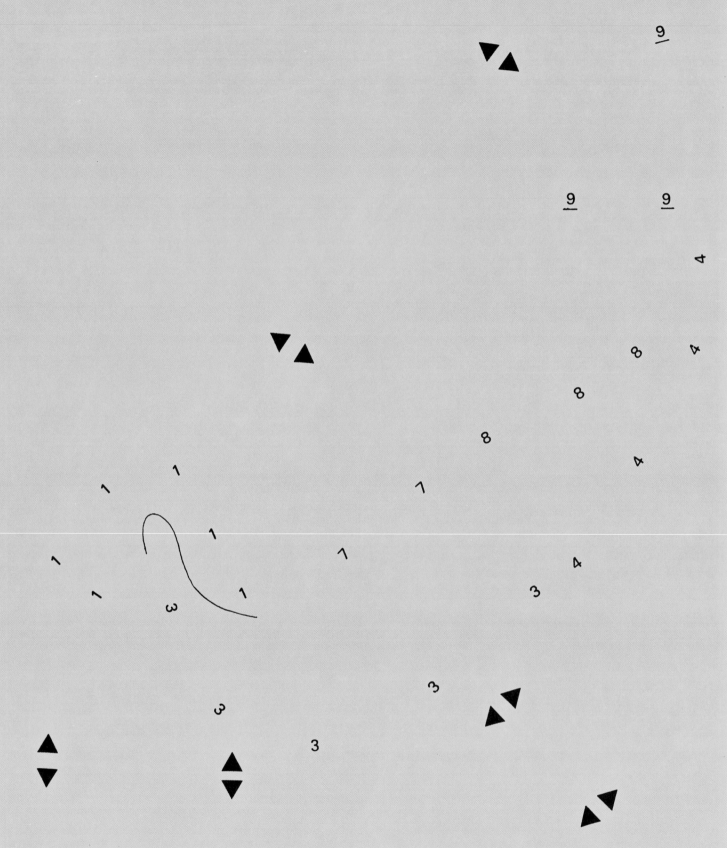

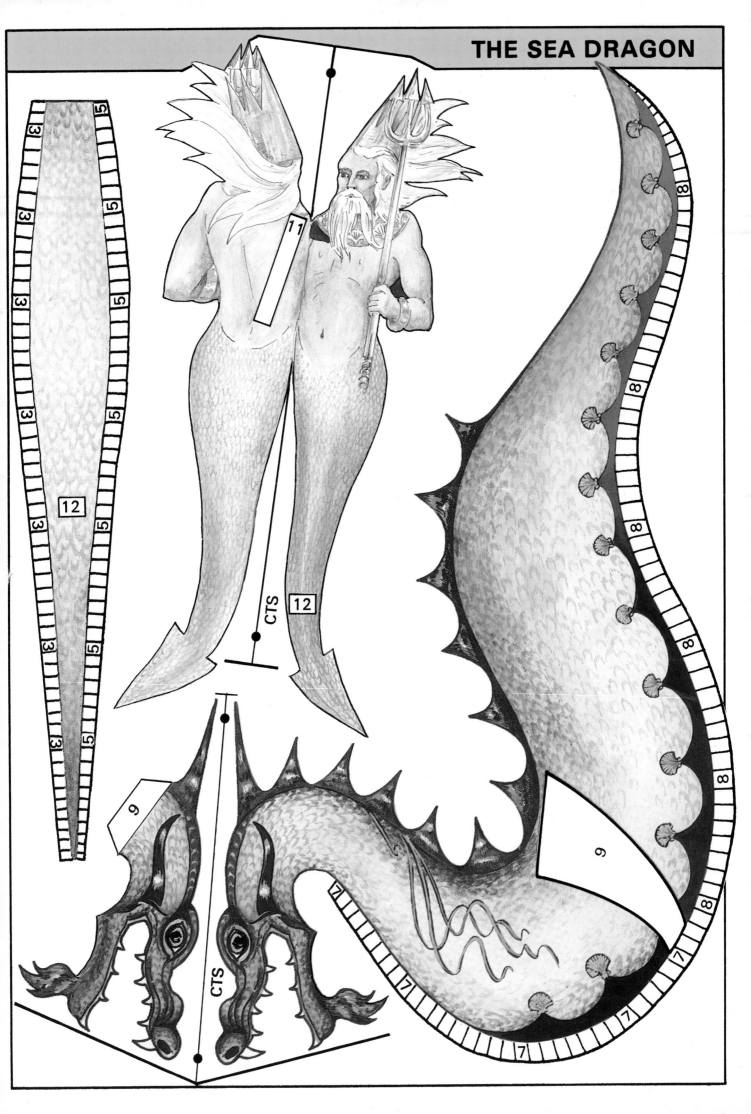

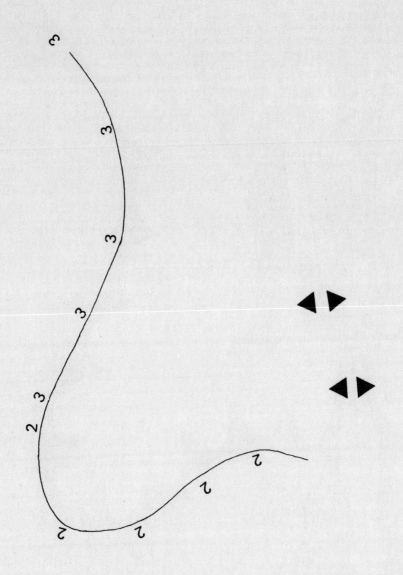

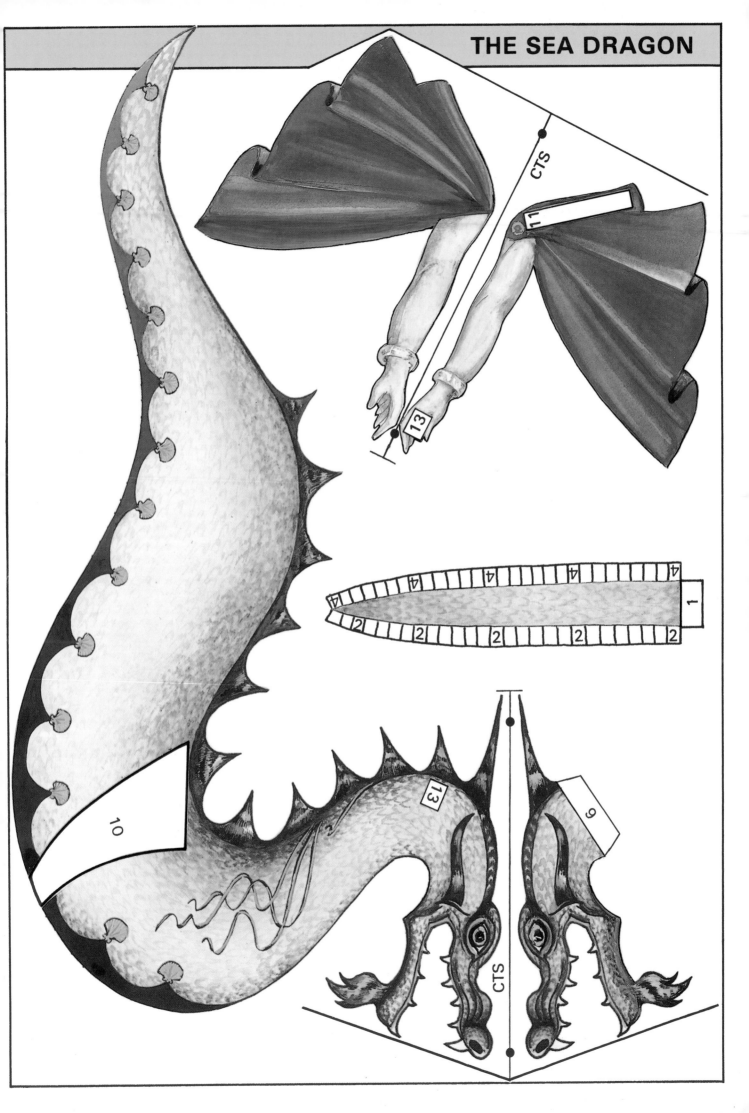

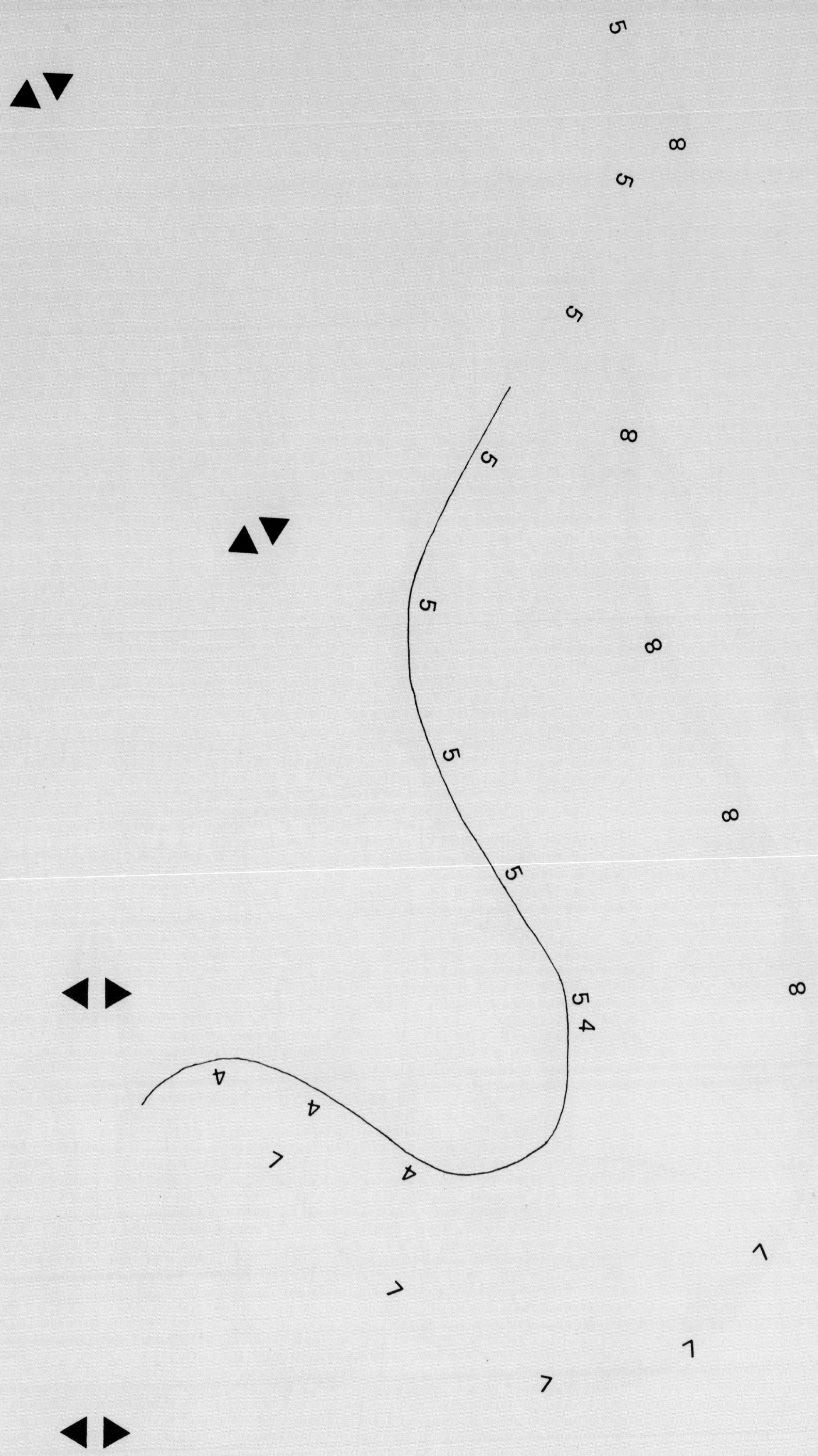

CTS

CTS

10

9

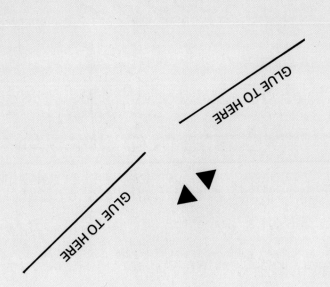

GLUE TO HERE

GLUE TO HERE

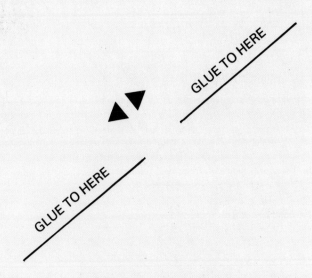

GLUE TO HERE

GLUE TO HERE